The Life and Work of
Mary
Cassatt

Ernestine Giesecke

www.heinemann.co.uk/library
Visit our website to find out more information about **Heinemann Library** books.

To order:
☎ Phone 44 (0) 1865 888066
▤ Send a fax to 44 (0) 1865 314091
 Visit the Heinemann Bookshop at www.heinemann.co.uk/library to browse our catalogue and order online.

First published in Great Britain by Heinemann Library, Halley Court, Jordan Hill, Oxford OX2 8EJ, part of Harcourt Education.
Heinemann is a registered trademark of Harcourt Education Ltd.

Editorial: Clare Lewis
Design: Jo Hinton-Malivoire and Q2A Creative
Production: Helen McCreath

Printed and bound in China by South China Printing Company

10 digit ISBN 0 431 09883 2
13 digit ISBN 978 0 431 09883 8

10 09 08 07 06
10 9 8 7 6 5 4 3 2 1

British Library Cataloguing in Publication Data
Giesecke, Ernestine
Life and Work of: Mary Cassatt - 2nd editon
759.1'3
A full catalogue record for this book is available from the British Library.

Acknowledgements
The publishers would like to thank the following for permission to reproduce photographs:
The Pennsylvania Academy of Fine Arts, Philadelphia, pp. 4, 8; The Denver Art Museum, Anonymous Bequest, p. 5; Drawing of Cassatt Family, Peter Baumgartner, 1854, Anonymous Owner, p. 6; Fine Arts Museums of San Francisco, Museum purchase, William H. Nobel Bequest Fund, 1979.35, p. 7; Founders Society Purchase, Robert H. Tannahill Foundation Fund, The Detroit Institute of Arts, p. 9; Corbis/Bettmann, p. 10; The Roland P. Murdock Collection, Wichita Art Museum, Wichita, Kansas, p.11; Bibliotheque Nationale, Department des Estampes, p. 12; Philadelphia Museum of Art, W.P. Wilstach Collection, p. 13; Erich Lessing/Art Resource, p. 14; Sterling and Francine Clark Art Institute, p. 15; The Bridgeman Art Library International, Ltd., pp. 16, 23; Collection of Mr. and Mrs. Paul Mellon, ©1999 Board of Trustees, National Gallery of Art, Washington, 1878, p.17; National Portrait Gallery, Smithsonian Institution. Gift of the Morris and Gwendolyn Cafritz Foundation and the Regents' Major Acquisitions fund, Smithsonian Institution, p. 18; The Metropolitan Museum of Art, Bequest of Edith H. Proskauer, 1975, p. 19; Anonymous Gift in Honor of Eugenia Cassatt Madeira

Cover photograph: *Self Portrait* by Mary Cassatt, reproduced with permission of National Portrait Gallery, Smithsonian Institution / Art Resource, NY.

The publishers would like to thank Nancy Harris for her assistance in the preparation of this book.

Every effort has been made to contact copyright holders of any material reproduced in this book. Any omissions will be rectified in subsequent printings if notice is given to the publishers.

The paper used to print this book comes from sustainable resources.

Some words in the book are bold, **like this**. You can find out what they mean by looking in the Glossary.

Contents

Who was Mary Cassatt?

Mary Cassatt was an American artist. She was a successful woman painter. This was at a time when most painters were men.

Most of Mary's art shows **scenes** from everyday life. Some of her best-known paintings are of mothers and children.

Early years

Mary was born on 22 May 1844 in Pittsburgh, USA. When Mary was seven years old she moved to Paris in France with her family. Later they moved to Germany. Mary was ten when this picture was drawn.

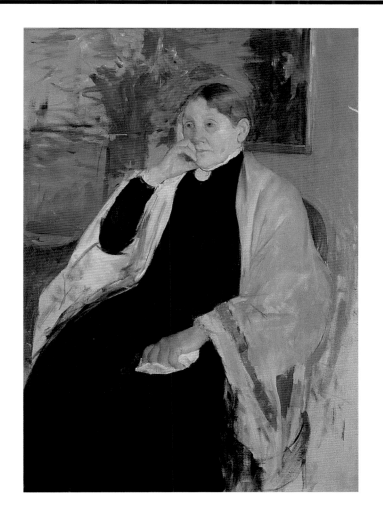

At school, Mary **studied** many subjects. She liked drawing and music. When Mary became an artist, she painted **portraits** of her family. This portrait shows her mother, Katherine Cassatt.

Philadelphia art student

In 1855 Mary and her family moved back to the United States. When Mary was 17 years old she went to the Pennsylvania Academy of Fine Arts. Mary is the girl on the right of the picture.

Mary learned to draw from life and by **studying** other works of art. She liked to ride horses with her older brother, Alexander. This is a **portrait** Mary painted of him when she was older.

Paris art student

When Mary was 21 years old, she travelled to Paris. She wanted to learn about art. She **studied** works of art by great artists. She copied paintings in a museum called the Louvre.

Mary studied **Madonna and Child** paintings. This helped her to paint her own pictures of mothers caring for their small children, like this one.

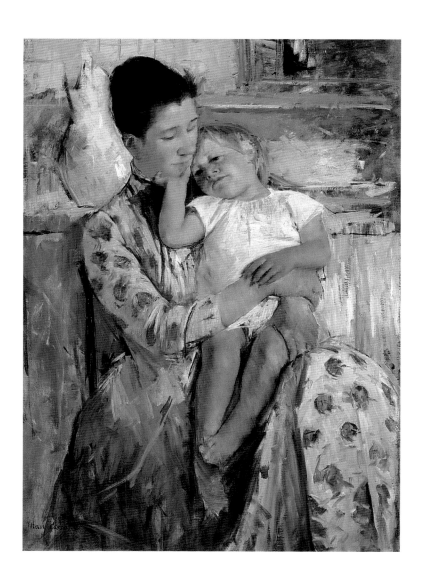

The Salon

In 1868 when Mary was 24 years old, her work was chosen to be shown in the **Salon** in Paris. The Salon was a place where artists who made excellent paintings showed their work.

This painting is called *On the Balcony during Carnival*. It is like many of the paintings Mary made when she first moved to Paris. It is the type of painting the Salon **judges** liked.

Professional artist

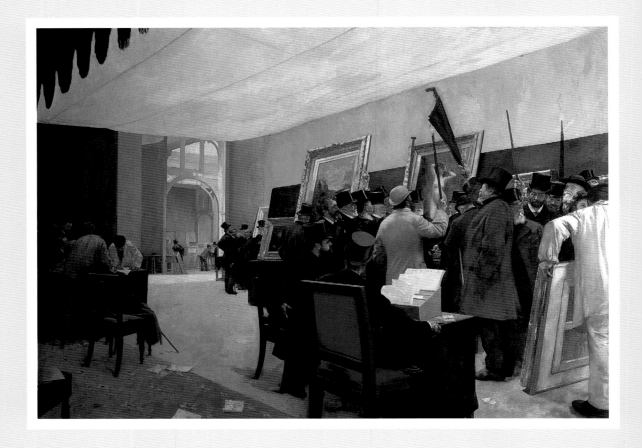

Mary **exhibited** in the **Salon** for a few more years. But she grew tired of having to paint what would please the **judges** at the Salon.

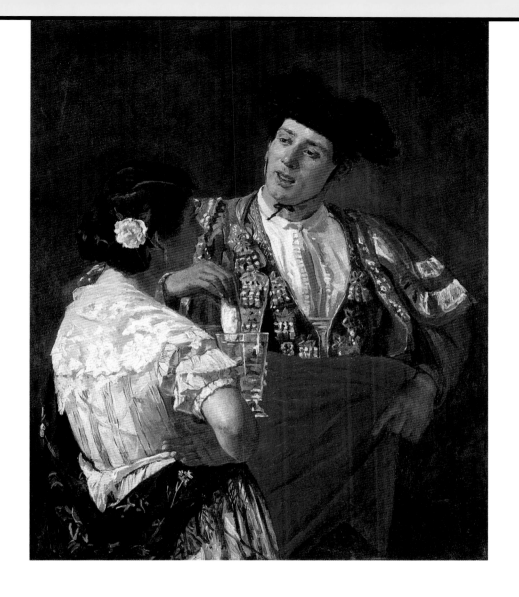

Mary did not want to paint **models** anymore. She did not want to use dark colours like in this painting. She wanted to paint things as she saw them.

15

Changing her ways

In 1877 Mary met another artist called Edgar Degas. Edgar introduced Mary to other painters. These painters were known as the **Impressionists**.
The Impressionists painted **scenes** of everyday life.

The Impressionists painted with **splotches** of colour. Mary liked the colours they used and the way they used them. She made this painting soon after she met Edgar.

Joining the Impressionists

Mary and Edgar became good friends. They visited each other's **studios**. They talked about their work. They gave each other ideas. Edgar Degas painted this **portrait** of Mary.

Mary used some of the **Impressionists'** ideas in her own paintings. She did this self-portrait in 1878. She used lighter colours and looser **brush strokes**.

Painting real life

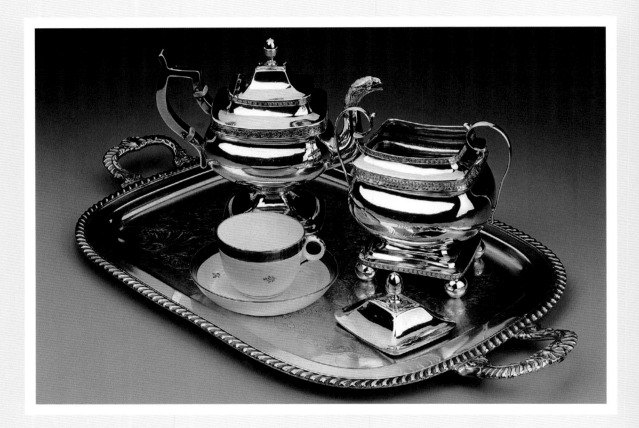

Most **Impressionists** painted outdoor **scenes**. Mary used the Impressionist ideas, but she painted indoor scenes. The paintings tell us about Mary's life.

Most of Mary's paintings are **portraits** of her family, friends, and neighbours. Many things in Mary's paintings belonged to her. Look at the silver tea set on page 20. You can see it in the painting on this page.

Painting women

Mary lived in a lively part of Paris near this café. Painters, musicians, and writers met at cafés to talk about their ideas. Mary and the women she knew read newspapers.

Mary sometimes painted women reading the newspaper. This was something new in painting. At that time, most artists painted **models** who **posed** just for the painting.

Mothers and children

Mary never married or had any children. Mary's brother, Alexander, and his family stayed with her when they visited Europe. Mary loved her nieces and nephews. She often painted pictures of them.

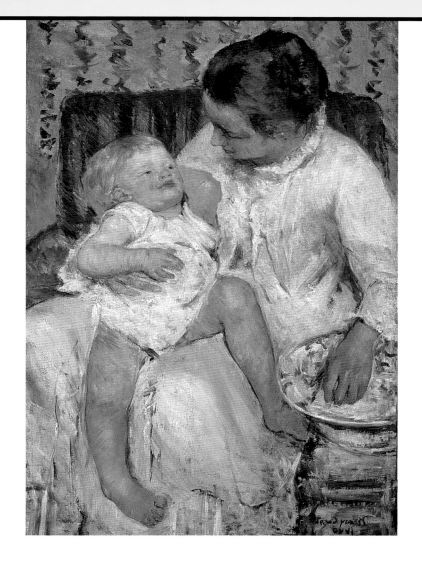

Mary spent hours on each drawing and painting. Yet much of her work shows scenes that would be over very quickly. This is a painting of a mother washing her sleepy child.

French countryside

Mary bought a house near Paris. She spent most of her time there. Her **studio** was on the first floor of her home. She could look out on to her pond and gardens.

This picture of ducks was **inspired** by the pond behind Mary's home. This picture is a print. A print allows an artist to make many copies of the same picture. Mary became very good at making prints.

A lasting impression

During the last years of Mary's life, her eyesight failed. She could not paint. Mary Cassatt died on 14 June 1926. She was 82 years old.

People still remember Mary Cassatt for her gentle pictures of mothers and children. She was important as a female artist because she was the only American to exhibit with the Impressionists.

Timeline

1844   Mary Cassatt is born on 22 May in Pittsburgh, USA.

1861   Mary begins her studies at Pennsylvania
          Academy of Fine Arts.

1865–70   Mary travels in Europe

1868   Mary's work first **exhibited** at the **Salon**.

1879   Mary exhibits with the **Impressionists**.

1893   Mary's first one-woman exhibition.

1900   World's Fair in Paris, France.

1914–18   The First World War.
          Mary moves to Italy to avoid the war.

1926   Mary Cassatt dies on 14 June.

Glossary

brush strokes marks left by an artist's paint brush

exhibit to show art in public

Impressionists group of artists who painted freely, showing light and movement

inspire to influence or guide

judge person who chose which pictures would be shown in the Salon

Madonna and Child work of art that shows Mary and baby Jesus

model person an artist paints or draws

portrait painting, drawing or photograph of a person

pose to sit or stand still for an artist

Salon place in Paris where artists were invited to show their artwork

scene place where something happens

splotch large spot

studio place where an artist works

study to learn about a subject

More books to read

Masterpieces: Mary Cassatt, Shelly Swanson Sateren (Franklin Watts, 2004)

The Children's Book of Art, Rosie Dickens (Usborne Publishing, 2005)

More paintings to see

The Sisters, Mary Cassatt, Glasgow Art Gallery, Glasgow

Young Woman Sewing in the Garden, Mary Cassatt, Musée d'Orsay, Paris

Mother and Child Against a Green Background, Mary Cassatt, Musée d'Orsay, Paris

Index